T0195966

PRAISE FOR
THERE ARE SECRETS TO TILING

As an owner of a successful interior design/renovation company of over twenty-two years, I always seek out the highest-quality artisans of their particular craft to make sure our customers are completely satisfied and our word-of-mouth reputation for outstanding work continues. I've worked with Rob for many years. His tiling knowledge and attention to detail are second to none. I am fully confident ... that he will do an exceptional job. His step-by-step approach to every facet of the job leaves nothing to chance. As a bonus, he goes out of his way to answer customer questions and help them understand the process, shepherding them through each step.

Rob's book gives you an excellent overview of the step-by-step process of tiling. He gives you various approaches to a beautiful end result.

Mark Jacobson
Jacobson Interiors
jacobsoninteriors.com

We have worked together with Rob for many years and have gotten to know him and his wonderful family personally. He is a hard and trustworthy worker, spiritually enlightened, and a truly honest and humble man. He is a loving father and husband—not to mention, an amazing master craftsman! He has also become a great author of many books of faith and, now, of this impressive book on tiling.

We are not surprised that Rob was willing to publish about his many years of work for all to read and learn from, as I have always known him to be a generous person. The book is very easy to read and understand for the layperson, as well as a great resource for people in the industry. It includes countless helpful hints and important things to know throughout any [tiling or grouting] project.

Andrea & Jeff Bowers
Tile Pro

There Are Secrets

—— to ——

TILING

The Best Way to Tile from Start to Finish

Rob Merines

Interior Image Credit: RGKNY Photography

Scripture taken from the New King James Version®. Copyright © 1982 by Thomas Nelson. Used by permission. All rights reserved.

The following brand and product names appearing in There Are Secrets to Tiling are trademarks of the respective trademark holders:

Durock
HardiBacker
Liquid Nails
OmniGrip Maximum Strength Tile Adhesive
RedGard
Schluter-DITRA
UltraLight Mold Tough Gypsum Board (green board)
Wonderboard

Note to the Reader: Due to differences in products, tools, and individual skills, the author assumes no responsibility for any damages, injuries suffered, or losses incurred as a result of following the instructions, advice, or other information published in this book. Before beginning any project, review the instructions carefully. If any doubts or questions remain, consult local experts or authorities. Codes and regulations vary by state and locality. Remember, always read and follow all of the safety precautions provided with any product, tool, or equipment manufacturer. Follow all generally accepted safety

Archway Publishing books may be ordered through booksellers or by contacting:

Archway Publishing
1663 Liberty Drive
Bloomington, IN 47403
www.archwaypublishing.com
1 (888) 242-5904

Because of the dynamic nature of the Internet, any web addresses or links contained in this book may have changed since publication and may no longer be valid. The views expressed in this work are solely those of the author and do not necessarily reflect the views of the publisher, and the publisher hereby disclaims any responsibility for them.

This book is a work of non-fiction. Unless otherwise noted, the author and the publisher make no explicit guarantees as to the accuracy of the information contained in this book and in some cases, names of people and places have been altered to protect their privacy.

ISBN: 978-1-4808-7616-3 (sc)
ISBN: 978-1-4808-7615-6 (e)

Library of Congress Control Number: 2019903346

Print information available on the last page.

Archway Publishing rev. date: 03/28/2019

CONTENTS

FOREWORD

Have you ever bought something that required assembly? I dislike such products intensely. Every time I have bought something and started to assemble it, I've had to put it together twice because I did not read the directions the first time. I'll find I've assembled it backward, missed a piece, or installed the wrong piece in the wrong place. But once I read and followed the directions, everything goes smoothly, and it looks great in the end.

If you follow the directions and recommendations in the pages that follow, on how to do a tiling job properly from start to finish, everything will look great at the end—and it won't take you as long to get to that point, either!

As in every industry, professional tile setters have developed extensive knowledge and many secrets, or keys to excellence. These consummate professionals have learned shortcuts and systems that serve them well in their day-to-day work. Often, they'll try to keep their tricks to themselves, but knowing some of those secrets can make your tiling job a lot easier.

Can you imagine knowing one of the best practitioners in the tiling trade and then revealing his secrets to you—before you lay a single tile?

In this book, you will discover numerous secrets to tiling that will help you in your next do-it-yourself project. If you are looking to start a career in tiling, or if you're a professional who just wants to refine your knowledge further, this book is for you, too.

There Are Secrets to Tiling is packed with insight, knowledge, and wisdom that Rob has gained over the years as a tiling contractor. Homeowners, do-it-yourselfers, and pros alike will benefit from these tricks of the trade Rob has acquired and is willing to share with the world.

Rob's greatest mission in life is to help others—his goal is to empower people to do a job well. In this handbook, he has truly made the art of tiling accessible to others in a simplified, step-by-step fashion.

And it all starts with planning.

—Alex Milan
Tile and Grout Pro

1

PLANNING

Everything starts with an idea. To paraphrase self-help writer Napoleon Hill, I have learned that you can achieve whatever your mind is capable of conceiving and believing.

After supper one evening, I said to my wife, "I'm building a bookshelf for my office!" In which she immediately responded, "Draw it out. I want to see it." She knew I had no drawing, but just a picture in my mind. So I immediately went to my toolbox and took out my engineer and architect scales, found some drawing paper, and started to map out the bookshelf I wanted to build.

I showed it to my wife, and she loved it. She was able to see the big picture; she could see all the dimensions, the size of the project, and the number of shelves it would have.

The beauty of having a drawing is that it's easy to make changes. Changes at this stage are made easily with a pencil and an eraser—and cheaper, too. You can't make changes after the project is complete because that would mean re-doing the whole project again. Can you make changes along the way? Absolutely! But why not plan it and map it out before you even start? It will save you a lot of time and money to plan your project out thoroughly.

Not only is it important to plan the project through drawing it out, but it is also important to plan what kinds of material you will use and how much you will be investing in the project. When doing something you want to last—something you want to enjoy for a long time—don't go cheap! Something cheap will definitely look cheap. In the long run, you will enjoy your finished project more, and if you're selling it, you will get your money's worth, if you decide to use high-quality materials instead of the cheaper options.

Oftentimes, when people go looking for tiles, they find the cheapest tile, buy it, and install it. A year later, they realize that they made a mistake buying something so cheap. They realize that if they had invested an extra 50¢ per tile, it would have made more of an impact on their floor—and, therefore, on the entirety of the room.

Planning any project goes a long way. It gives you reference points and an idea of how the project will turn out.

MEASUREMENTS

Part of planning is figuring out how much material you will need. When determining your tile count, always add 10% for waste and cuts.

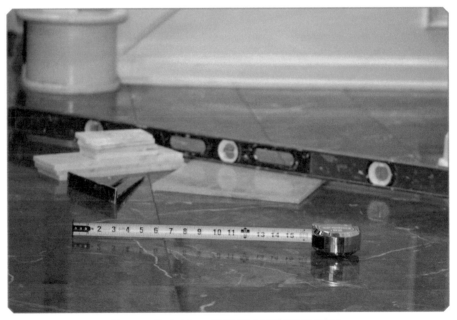

Preparation pays—Drawing and measuring.

It is also important to consider how much thinset mortar you will need. When spreading thinset, I recommend using a ½" trowel to make it easier to level the tiles. When using a ½" trowel, you will need two 50-lb. bags for 100 square ft. If the floor or wall is a little uneven in some places, you will need 2.5 bags of thinset for every 100 ft.^{2} of tile covering. For example, if you are doing 300 ft.^{2} of tile floor covering, you need 7.5 bags of thinset—so you would buy 8 bags, as stores do not sell half-bags.

To work out the number of bags required, you just multiply 2.5 bags by 3. In this example, 2.5 represents the number of bags per 100 ft. and the 3 represents 300 feet.

Again, any time you take planning measurements for any tile work, add 10% of the total number for waste and cuts. That way, you are not running back and forth between the project site and the store to get more tiles. It is better to have too much material than too little, and you can always return unused materials. It is also a good idea to keep a few extra tiles just in case you need to replace one or two in the future.

2

CHOOSING THE RIGHT MATERIALS

Of course, all of the planning in the world won't help you if you aren't using the right materials of sufficient quality.

Two options are the most common materials to choose from when prepping a floor: drypack and Durock. Drypack is the old way of preparing a subfloor for tiling, while Durock is one of the most recent and popular materials to become available for prepping a subfloor. Next, I will discuss them in greater detail—beginning with drypack.

DRY PACK

Installing dry pack on shower floor after durock.

I began working with a tile setter in Long Island, New York, in 1995. I was both thrilled and intrigued on my first day as a tiler's helper.

That's when I encountered dry pack for the first time. What is dry pack? It is a mixture of Portland cement and sand, (or sand mix) and it's the right material for any sub floor. Many retailers sell it in 60–80-lb. bags that are already mixed.

In our case, we had to mix the sand and cement with water to make the dry pack. It's mixed in such a way that it's not too wet and not too dry. If you can grab it with your hand and it doesn't break or slide, then it is perfect to work with. You can level it better if it's semi-dry rather than too wet. Wet mix will sink in and is hard to work with.

Perfect mixed dry pack.

This process takes time, and it's relatively messy and expensive. Not a lot of tile-setting professionals offer this kind of process, and not a lot of customers want to pay the price for it, either.

Dry pack is mainly used on large floors. And we always use it on shower floors after the lining and durock are installed.

Dry and ready to tape and waterproof.

I recommend the dry pack process for large floors where the subfloor is not too strong.

The last project I did using dry pack was in a sunroom. While the customer wanted something fast and inexpensive, I recommended the dry pack process because the subfloor was a wooden deck and not very steady. If I had not used dry pack, the grout and tiles would have broken in a fairly short time.

We first had to prepare the floor by securing the wood with deck screws. Then we installed felt roof deck protection paper as a vapor barrier, followed by steel lath for strength. After that, the dry pack was ready to be installed.

When you're installing dry pack, it needs to be leveled—in particular, it needs to be leveled with the floor. Its thickness can range from ½" to 1" depending on how strong it needs to be. The professional I was learning from in New York set a 1-ft.^{2} corner with dry pack. Once he had leveled that portion of the floor at the thickness he wanted, he laid down dry pack for the rest of the floor, using an 8-ft. level to level it as he went. The result was a perfectly leveled floor that was ready to have tile installed on it.

Spreading and leveling dry pack seems like a lot of work, and it is, but there is a secret to doing it: making rails. For example, if the room is 12 ft. by 16 ft., install three 1" by 1" by 8 ft., premium square edge whitewood common boards (rails). Place them in three lines—one on each side of the room, and one in the middle, making two rows. Now you can spread the dry pack one row at a time. When leveling it, slide a two-by-four on the rails to even out the dry pack. After it is dry, normally by the following day, take out the rails and fill in the tracks with dry pack.

Installing dry pack is more time-consuming, but it is worth doing. If you want a long-lasting, perfectly leveled floor that is free of broken tile and grout, then dry pack is the way to go. The secret to using dry pack is creating a strong, level base beneath the tiles. The final result is a strong, level tiled floor.

DUROCK CEMENT BOARD

Half of all tile setters seem to have no idea what dry pack is; therefore, they do not offer it.

Besides dry pack, Durock is the first choice of homeowners and contractors to tile shower walls and floors—mostly because it's faster and inexpensive to install. This works well when the sub floor is properly prepared. I highly recommend Durock for floors and walls because it is 100% cement, it has no fillings, and its nylon mesh adds even more strength. It absorbs water and will neither dissipate nor break once it's installed.

Many people use UltraLight Mold Tough Gypsum Board, best known as green board, because it's cheaper and is easy to install wall tiles on. However, here is a secret regarding green

Durock installed after plywood is prepared—is is best to tape joints.

board: it is the same as sheetrock, except that it is green and mold-resistant, which makes it perfect for bathroom walls outside of the shower.

People make the mistake of installing green board on shower walls. Sadly, green board is not designed for shower walls. There's a lot of water exposure on the shower, so over time, as the green board gets exposed to water—especially on the bottom of the shower wall—it will dissolve and tiles will start to fall. Time after time, I've been hired to repair shower walls with disintegrated green board because there was a small grout gap and water had made its way through. In short, it's critical not to use green board on shower walls.

I have also done many wall repairs where there was leakage through cracked grout and Durock was underneath. The Durock was strong, and it was only damp; it just needed to dry before tiling.

Durock is an excellent product and, in my opinion, the best choice to use on shower walls and floors. In my experience, green board and another product, which I hesitate even to name (it's HardieBacker) produce inferior results.

If the board is not 100% cement, I don't recommend using it. Whether it's 90% or 50% cement, I will not use it. Durock is the way to go. You will learn more about Durock and how to install as we go along.

SCHLUTER-DITRA SYSTEM

I have only work with Schluter-DITRA once. Does it work? Absolutely—but again, the sub floor needs to be prepared, as if you were going to install dry pack or Durock. If the sub floor is unprepared, the Schluter-DITRA system will not work.

I have done some repairs on Ditra where the floor underneath was not properly prepared. If you use this produce, be sure to read and follow the directions on how to install it.

THINSET

When choosing a thinset mortar, don't use the cheapest one. A good thinset will cost you between $16 and $25 for a 50 lb bag. Do not use a thinset that costs less than $10 because it will require an additive for strength—and this will cost you just as much as if you'd bought the more expensive product to begin with.

A decent-quality thinset is rigid. If the quality is inferior, you will see movement. I recommend using a Non-slumping formula to eliminates lippage.

TILES

Nowadays, there are tons of tiles to choose from. What tiles to pick?

They are available in a virtually unlimited array of colors, styles, shapes, patterns, and sizes. Whatever finished look you have in mind, you can easily find the right tile for it. A properly planned, laid out, and installed tiled floor makes a powerful statement.

Remember to design and draw the tile pattern the way you want it to look before you install your first tile.

Porcelain tile—with natural stone appearance.

In my opinion, if you want a maintenance-free tile, get porcelain tiles. Natural stone, such as travertine, marble, or tumble marble, looks beautiful but requires a lot more maintenance than porcelain. Regular ceramic tiles are not too strong, but porcelain is stronger, and there are so many great-looking options. You can even find porcelain tiles that look like wood!

Rectangular porcelain tile with 1/8" grout line.

Again, I would recommend staying away from natural stones, especially for the shower floor, because natural stone is porous. It has veins and grains, so over time, water gets behind it and water damage starts to show up.

I once gutted my master shower walls and floor, installing tumble marble—natural stone. It required a lot of maintenance, and after five years of use, some shower floor tiles had broken. Water got behind them, so I had to remove the shower floor tiles. Luckily, the dry pack underneath was not damaged, so I just restored and reinforced the base with mortar. Then I applied RedGard waterproofing and installed new tiles. Another five years later and the new tiles are still perfect!

The other type of tile to avoid installing in the shower floor is glass tile. Glass tiles look beautiful, but they are designed for walls. They are mostly used on accent walls and backsplashes, and they are unsuitable for floors.

SHOW ROOMS

I tell my customers that if they go to show rooms, they may see a variety of beautiful designs that wouldn't work on all projects. However, if you can envision your tile needs, tile retailers can help you make your vission a reality. Tile show-rooms, stores and warehouses like The Home Depot, with their quality tile and natural stone selections, offer you virtually endless options to create new rooms or upgrade existing ones.

Design services are not as expensive as you may think. Infact, at most tile stores, they 're free. You'll find that dedicated proffecionals are ready to discuss your tiling ideas and offer suggestions about arragements, materials, and maintenance to help you create your dream room from start to finish.

Keep in mind that not all tiles are made equally. All tiles have a bow—it's normal. However, some tiles' bowing is so severe that I strongly recommend not buying them, no matter how little they cost. Severely bowed tiles will create lippage, or unevenness across the tiled surface. You can easily spot excessive bowing just by looking at the tiles.

Porcelain wall tile and river rocks on shower floor.

Regardless of what sort of tiles you decide on, no matter what size they're labeled, they will differ subtly in size, and these variations will affect the grout line. As installers, we try our best to align the grout lines, but one tile may be a bit bigger or smaller than the others, which messes up the line slightly. Typically, the installer doesn't see this immediately, but after the tile has dried, it becomes visible.

Some people like to see a lot of grout line; others like to see less. The most common grout line size is ⅛". To me personally, this is the best grout line size. Not too big and not too small—it's just right!

3
PREPARATION

Good preparation is the biggest secret to making a job go smoothly. In the case of large and detailed jobs, this can mean days of preparation. First, check the room you are working on to see how square and straight the walls are, how even and smooth the edges appear to be, and how level the floor and walls are.

Once you've established this, begin to work out your preparation methods. For uneven floors, using self-leveling compound works wonders. This works well because you just mix it in a 5-gallon bucket. Mix it to a watery consistency and just release it onto the surface; it will automatically fill the unleveled areas. If you are leveling a severely unlevel wooden floor, I recommend installing a piece of steel lath for extra strength and to avoid breakage of the self-leveling material.

Preparation can take longer than the actual tiling, but it's definitely worthwhile. Not only will the tiling process go smoothly, but you'll have a much better outcome as well.

Take your time to prepare the room or wall thoroughly, looking out for any obstruction along the way to avoid wasting time. Before you start tiling, all preparation must be complete and done well.

Preparation of the floor to replace damaged plywood.

To recap from the previous chapter, it is always a good idea to draw out and otherwise plan your project clearly. If you try to incorporate more elements as you go, the project will take too much time. In fact, if you forgot to plan for a shower niche for your shampoo from the outset, it will take you twice as much time to add it along the way. The same applies if you need a corner bench.

I have lost so much time when the project is in progress and the customer wants to add a niche. Luckily, on one such occasion, the tiles were not up yet—just the Durock. Substantial amounts of time were spent figuring out the measurements, and cutting and framing the box. However, if the tile had been up already, it would have been too late to add a niche. You can only add a corner shelf at that point in time.

You can also install a small premade corner bench if needed. It just needs to be bolted against the finished tile, then tiled and grouted. Installing this premade corner bench has worked well with all of my installations. They come in either plastic or metal—I prefer the plastic one because it is easier to work with when tiling.

FLOOR FAILURE

Many people complain about the grout breaking in their floor. The reason is not a poor tile layout or poor tiling work. It is the lack of preparation.

The reason why the grout is breaking is because the plywood moves, and you'll hear a squeaky noise when you walk on the tiled floor. There is nothing you can do except to remove the tiles and start over. Yes, you can re-grout it, but it will keep breaking.

Why does the plywood move? Because when it was originally installed, it was installed with nails, using a nail gun for a faster job. There's nothing wrong with that, necessarily, but over the years, the joist became dry and the nail holes expanded. As a result, the nail loosened, allowing the plywood to shift. Some contractors know that this will happen, so they also add Liquid Nails. This is an adhesive to glue the plywood against the joist or beam. In reality, though, the plywood needs to be screwed down. You can hear the squeaky noises when you walk in any room, whether carpeted, hardwood, or even tiled. The problem was not addressed before installing the floor covering.

The proper way to fix this is to find the beam and fasten the plywood with deck screws. Don't use

Grout breaking in the middle of floor due to poor preparation.

sheetrock or drywall screws; they break easily because they are not strong enough for plywood. Use deck screws because they are stronger and will not break. Once the plywood is secure, you will feel that the subfloor is stronger and firmer. After installing screws all over the floor, walk around to see if you hear any squeaky noise—if you do, install more screws and be sure that each screw is tight with the beam.

Once this step is done, you are now ready to install Durock (or whatever sub floor you choose).

INSTALLING DUROCK

In this section, I will discuss the installation of Durock, also known as cement board. While there is another kind of board called HardieBacker, I wholly prefer Durock. As I said previously, if the board you are using is not 100% cement, it will deteriorate.

Here is an example: Have you seen a driveway washed away? Have you seen a driveway consumed with so much water it has become soft? Have you seen a driveway deteriorate or break? Unless the foundation is weak and tree roots are growing under it, the driveway should resist wind, rain, snow, etc. This is why cement is important—because it can withstand all elements. Cement will withstand and resist any water or humidity in any place of installation.

This is one of the most significant secrets of my company over my twenty years of service. In these two decades, I have only installed material that was not Durock once. My team and I have never had a problem with grout breaking or poor layout because we take the time to prepare the area and do the job right the first time.

So, why else should you consider using Durock? Because Durock is the primary material, other than dry pack, that homeowners and installers prefer. It's fast, clean, and cheaper than the dry pack. Durock will work great when installed properly.

Installing Durock and taping with white thinset.

How do you properly install and prepare Durock so that it will have a long-lasting life?

Well, first off, sheets of Durock only come in one size and three different thicknesses. Its size, or its area, is a 3-ft. by 5-ft. sheet, and its thickness can be ¼", ½", or ¾", the latter of which is not too common. Most retailers do not stock the ¾", so it usually has to be preordered.

WHEN SHOULD YOU USE EACH THICKNESS?

Let's say, for example, that you are tiling a kitchen floor that is ¾" lower than the rest of the floors. For this, you can use the ¼" Durock, leaving the floor ½" lower. Most tile thickness is a little more than ¼", plus thinset, so in this example, your new tile floor will be at the same level, or flush, with the other floors. This means you will not need a threshold, or transition, dividing the floors. This is a well-prepared job!

In many cases, the tile could be almost ½" in thickness. If this is the case, then use the ¼" Durock. If the floors are carpeted, then always use ½" Durock. It will come out level with the carpet.

Some people like to put in a marble, wood, or metal threshold, or transition, either way. At this point, it is a matter of preference. But you need to know whether or not you will use a threshold beforehand so you can make adjustments before the tile layout process. The common marble threshold comes in two widths 2" and 4"and its length is 36".

4" wide marble threshold or transition dividing both tile and wood floors.

When installing Durock, install the sheets across the beams for more strength. I also recommend spreading Liquid Nails to give the plywood and Durock added strength. Liquid Nails is a form of glue that comes in tubes, similar to caulking tubes. The Liquid Nails must be applied between the plywood and Durock. That way, you will not have any movement, and this will also prevent the grout from breaking in the future.

When installing Durock, there are certain screws that you should use. Do not—seriously, do not—install Durock with drywall screws. Use the screws made especially for Durock. When you buy the Durock at your favorite store, you will likely find them right next to the Durock. If not, ask the sales associates.

Durock screws.

Do not use the HardieBacker screws on Durock, and don't use Durock screws on HardieBacker—they don't work well. I have seen people install Durock screws on HardieBacker, and the screw heads stick up. HardieBacker screws are usually green. Durock screws are typically grey in color.

PREPARING WALLS

On shower walls, grout breaking typically does not occur in the middle of the wall. It usually occurs in the corners, around the tub, or around shower stalls. Again, this happens because of poor preparation.

You see, once an inexperienced tiler finishes installing the Durock, they begin tiling immediately, thinking that installing Durock is all they need to do—but it is not. When you leave the corners unprepared, not only does the grout break, but water starts to seep in through those gaps and makes its way to the ceiling below. Soon after these cracks occur, you will likely notice a water stain on the ceiling.

When preparing walls, check for concaved or uneven studs. Sometimes it is easier to replace the uneven stud than to shave it with an electrical planer. Many bathrooms are poorly framed, especially at the corners. It is always good to reinforce the corners where the Durock will meet by adding extra studs on each side.

Often, in the middle of the wall, the studs are set too far apart. If the original installer framed it at 20"–24" apart instead of the code 16" on center, it is always a good idea to add an extra stud in the middle of both for extra strength and wall stability. Then, when installing Durock, it will feel stronger and more secure.

Reinforce improperly framed walls.

HOW TO PREPARE DUROCK ON WALLS

A lot of installers do not tape the shower wall corners, which is why grout starts breaking there.

Just like with any drywall, if the installers do not tape and spackle the corners of walls and ceilings, the corners will break. As when preparing shower walls, cement board joint tape needs to be installed. This tape is available at most retailers. Otherwise, you can use self-adhesive mesh drywall joint tape. It is strong and will work well.

When using alternative tape, use meshed tape, not paper tape. After installing the tape, mud it with thinset (do not use drywall compound). Use the same thinset you will use for tiling. Let it dry, and use waterproof on the corners for extra strength (and waterproofing). Though waterproofing will cost more, it is worth installing because you will not have cracked grout anymore. Personally, I tape all corners, including the floor corners, curbs and niches, to avoid grout breakage there as well. I have gone back to work other jobs where I have previously installed bathrooms, and their shower still looks brand new, with no grout problems. That's a point of pride for me personally and for our company.

Therefore, to prevent breakage of grout, I recommend taping all corners. It will only take you 45 minutes to an hour to do.

Shower walls and floor ready to waterproof

Taping corners on shower walls, and shower floor.

19

INSTALLING WATERPROOF

Waterproofing is vital in any shower preparation. On shower walls, the water hits at about 36" (3 ft.) off the floor, so I do not waterproof the complete walls—I just install waterproof 3–4 ft. from the floor.

Instead of applying it all the way, I apply it at the corners. When I waterproof corners, I only apply it 3" wide on each side for added protection. However, I waterproof all of the shower floor. Waterproofing the shower floor works well because if the floor tile fails, the water does not penetrate the cement. Then you'll only need to change tiles and not the cement floor or dry pack beneath it.

With every job I do, I keep this one thing above all in mind:

> And whatever you do, do it heartily,
> as to the Lord and not to men.
> —Colossians 3:23

This is the foundation of my business model. I teach this scripture to my employees, and we have been blessed and found tremendous success by it.

Applying waterproof after taping is completely dry.

4
LAYOUT

FLOOR LAYOUT

Before you install the first tile, you need to determine the layout of the floor space in which you're working. Begin by figuring out the CL, or center line, of the room you are tiling. This is necessary to be sure that the tiled floor will have an even and symmetrical appearance.

If you are doing a rectangular or square floor, the CL will be easy to locate. It becomes more difficult when you have other shapes within the floor, such as those created by closets, islands, cabinets, or walls. For these situations, you need to look at the layout and anticipate where the edge of the tile is going to run or end up.

You can use a chalk line to make lines parallel or perpendicular from the center line, or where the edges of other walls end.

A laser level could be handy and useful at this point as well. If you don't have a laser level, however, a chalk line will do the job. You can create as many lines as you like until you have a perfect floor layout. Play around with it until you have the layout you are looking for.

For rectangular or square shapes, first lay out a run of tiles with spacers (without thinset), just to see how it will look. Do this from the center line toward

A non-square floor space.

one side, either the left or the right side of the room. Remember to include spacers. This will let you know if you'll end up with a sliver around the room edges. If that's the case, you can make adjustments so the sliver don't occur.

For example, if you end up with half or ¾ of a tile, the outcome will be perfect because you will have an equal cut on both ends. You will have a symmetrical-looking floor. But if you end up with a 2" or 4" strip or sliver of tile, that cut is too small, and the outcome will look awful. In any floor installation, if you see a small cut, it doesn't look good; that indicates a poor layout.

The way you make an adjustment is to take the same run of tile and find the center of the tile. Now lay down the tile (without thinset) center to center, meaning you put the center of the tile on the center line. Lined up center to center, lay down the tiles to one side of the center (adding spacers), and you will find out what you'll end up with. You should now have a bigger cut at the outside edge, which is what you want. You are looking to have a piece no smaller than half of a tile.

Do the same procedure length-wise. That way, you will know how the finished product will look before installing—which is why we work on the layout prior to any installation.

Once the center line is determined and the layout marked out, tiling begins.

WALL LAYOUT

When it comes to tiling walls, use the same process for each individual wall. If the tiles are going to be straight or a brick pattern, measure and find the CL for each individual wall. Again, figure out how big or small the ends are going to be, both horizontally and vertically, and be sure to avoid having a sliver of tile at the top, bottom, or sides for a better-looking outcome. Also, be sure to find out if the walls are squared, leveled, or plumed. For the most part, they are rarely ever leveled or plumed, which is why it is always good to leave room for trimming tiles.

It is rare for a room's walls to be square, but if that is the case, you may lay out a row of tile with spacers just to check. You could end up with a full tile at both ends. Then, you can lay out the full tile and start tiling without worrying that you may end up with an uneven gap or a sliver at the other end of the wall.

Sliver is too small—poor layout.

If you are doing a diamond or diagonal layout, find the CL of one wall. Diagonal installation is little tricky. It takes more time and more product because there are twice as many cuts and there is much more waste. When you start laying the tile, select a wall and continue the grout lines across all of the walls for even, straight grout lines. You need to follow the same diagonal line to the next wall.

Diagonal installation needs to follow same grout line on all walls.

That same line needs to follow all around in a continual manner. The end of one wall and the end of the cut will determine the next piece on the following walls as you follow the same lines from wall to wall.

BACKSPLASH LAYOUT

Use the same technique when tiling a backsplash. Find the CL of each individual wall and figure out how you will end up on the sides. When it comes to the bottom and the top, start with a full tile on the bottom and work your way up. For the most part, you don't need to worry about how big or small the piece on top ends up being; it's hardly seen, anyway, and all customers are fine with that.

Backsplash tiling—different sections.

I always start with a full tile on the bottom because a cut tile doesn't look good at the bottom. Most countertops are level, so you don't need to level the tiles, and you can start with a full tile from the bottom up. If the countertop is not level, then trim the tile to follow the level line.

Also, for the most part, people use small tiles on backsplashes, which turns out well. Glass tile is the preferred option for backsplashes today. They come on a 12-ft. by 12-ft. sheet, and you scarcely need to lay them out to envision the results. Because they are small, thin pieces glued to the net that holds them together, I usually start gluing them from the beginning of the wall to the end of the wall.

For glass cutting, you ideally want a glass blade, but most of the time, a regular blade will cut them just as well. Test the regular blade first—if the cut is rough, then get the glass-cutting blade. They are available at your favorite retailer. When cutting glass or any tile, make sure you wear goggles.

Cut tiles around electric box, leaving the outlet room to grab on to the tile.

One other thing to remember when doing backsplashes is to unscrew the electrical outlet and pull it out as needed. Do not disconnect the outlet; just pull it out. As you are tiling around it, make sure you cut the tile right at the edge of the electrical outlet box, leaving room for the outlet's ears to grab onto the tile.

Loosen screws to tile around the outlet box.

When the outlet is put back, it needs to grab the tile; otherwise, there will be a problem with holding the outlet in place. Therefore, avoid cutting the tile too far from the outlet box so that the outlet doesn't sink in when put back.

Also, when cutting the tile hole for the electric box, if you are installing tiles on a net, cut the net in half and then cut the space where the outlet box will go. It is easy to make the cut on a half tile rather than making the cut on the whole tile. This will save you lots of time, too.

5

TILE INSTALLATION

TOOLS YOU NEED TO START TILING

- Manual tile cutter
- Wet tile saw
- ½" trowel for thinset
- $^1/_{16}$" or ⅛" trowel for adhesive
- Flat-margin trowel
- Variable-speed oscillating multi-tool (to cut around door trim)
- Grinder with a tile blade
- Grout spacers
- Thinset mortar
- Thinset mortar mixer
- 5-gallon bucket to mix thinset
- Knee pads

When tiling, never use ceramic tile adhesive to glue down the floor because it takes too long to dry and it is not designed for floor installation. It should only be used for walls. Also, never use thinset to grout tiles because it will wash away. Thinset is not designed for grouting.

CLEAN SURFACE

Before you start tiling, make sure you have the layout you want. Also, prior to tiling, make sure the surface is clean and clear of any debris and dust. For best results, use a vacuum.

FLOOR TILING

Knowing the measurements and where the tile will end from the layout, you can begin installing tiles from anywhere in the room—preferably ending near a doorway, allowing you to exit the room without stepping on the tiles. If you step on a freshly laid tile, it will sink and thinset will spill out from the back of the tile. If a tile has set for 3 to 4 hours, the thinset hasn't hardened enough; if you step on it, the tile will come loose from the thinset. I recommend not stepping on it until the following day, or after 12–24 hours.

For a comfortable and manageable rhythm, apply mortar to approximately 4–5 ft.^{2} at a time. Any more than that and chances are, the thinset will start to dry and the tiles won't stick to it.

Again, avoid boxing yourself in so that you have room to exit without stepping on the tile.

Here's a good example of how not to box yourself in: If you are working on a rectangular or square room, start tiling on one side of the room, going from front to rear, laying one row at a time. Once you get to the middle of the room, you can move and continue tiling at the end of the room. Then work yourself up to the front—that way there will be no obstruction.

Tiling started from the front; the wood and new tile floor came out flush. No need for a transition piece

Also, when cutting tile with a wet saw, make sure the tile is not wet or dripping water before you install it. Dry the water off of the tile because if the tile is wet, the thinset will reject it and will not stick to the tile. Get a rag and wipe off the water from the tile—then install.

LEVEL TILES AGAINST TILES

I highly recommend, when installing tiles and spreading thinset, to use a ½" trowel, which is wide and deep; you will use more mortar, but it works best for leveling the tiles. When you use more thinset, the job will flow more smoothly and it'll be easier to level the tiles. Remember, when you are tiling, you need to level the tile against the previous one.

Have you seen jobs where the tiles are uneven? It looks horrible! This is the result of poor workmanship—often a consequence of hiring an inexperienced setter, perhaps because of a desire for cheap labor.

If you want a cleaner, better-looking outcome when setting tiles, keep a bucket with water and a grout sponge close at hand to remove any excess thinset that has gone into the grout lines or onto the surface of the tile before it cures. If you don't clean as you go, this excess thinset will harden and you will spend more time removing it the following day. Be sure to place spacers on all sides of the tiles to maintain the consistency of the grout lines and to avoid tiles joining together and losing grout size.

Level tiles against previously laid tiles.

TILE CUTTING

The edges of most walls are not straight. To cut tiles for the edge of a wall, measure one end of the tile, including the spacer, and mark it with a pencil. Next, measure the other end of the tile, mark it, and draw a line at the mark. Then cut and install. A hand dry cutter will be useful at this time. Dry cutters save a lot of time.

When cutting with the dry cutter, mark the tile right where you will cut and insert it in the cutter, holding it firm. Then run the cutter handle to the back and slide it from back to front once. Keep holding the tile firmly; then press down, and the tile will divide into two pieces. The key here is not to move the tile while sliding the cutter. If it shifts, the chances are that the tile will not cut. Also, only run the blade once.

For uneven cuts, meaure both ends and then cut.

Cutting uneven or unusual shapes can result in a lot of wasted material, especially when cutting diagonally. The best way to deal with this is to find a piece of paper (it could be newspaper), cut the paper to the size of the tile, place the paper where the tile will go, and make a template of that area. Then take that template, trace it onto the tile, and cut the tile. You will end up with a perfect cut and shape.

CURING TIME

Prior to applying grout and stepping on the newly installed tiles, read the manufacturer's required curing time for the thinset used. Some types of thinset dry faster than others.

To be safe, don't step on the tiles until the next day. Most jobs are ready to grout the next day.

WALL TILE INSTALLATION

Again, when installing wall tile, you need a layout, and you need to find the center line (CL).

Every time I tile walls, I use a temporary ledger board at the bottom of the shower wall, leaving space to fill in the very bottom of the wall as the last tile row. Just make sure you level it! Only use a perfectly straight piece of wood. How to start, measure the hight of the tile from the lowest point of the floor—that is your level point. Place your level across that point, mark it, and install the ledger boards below the leveled mark, if you decide to use them.

Remember to screw this ledger where the studs are; be careful with the water lines. I use this process because it's faster than trying to level each tile from the floor to the level line, and the result is much more level overall.

Now set your first row of tiles directly on the piece of wood, with no spacers underneath. This way, the weight from all of the rows of tile has something solid to rest against while the thinset is curing.

When the tiles are dry, usually the following day, I then remove the wood and cut or trim the remaining lower tiles one by one, leaving a perfectly level cut.

Temporary ledger board, removed the following day when other tiles are dry.

Keep in mind that the weight from the tiles is only a concern during the setting of the tile. Once the thinset has dried, you can remove the ledger board and complete the final row.

TILING AROUND TUBS

When tiling around a tub, start from the lowest point of the tub, not from the highest point. This is because the tub is never level. As you look at tubs, the side of the drain slopes down; the opposite side is higher. If you look at old tiling jobs, you will frequently notice mistakes because the installer did not check the height or level of the tub and started tiling anywhere.

When choosing to start somewhere other than the lowest point, you'll likely come across to the other side and realize you need a ¼" or even ¾" longer tile because the tub edge is lower than the tiling point where you started. It is then difficult to remove the previous tiles, especially if a full wall was completed. They can still be moved, but that involves reverting to demolition, which will delay your work.

Some people choose not to start the project over again, and they just leave the error. They apply ¼" to ½" of grout to a gap that should have been ⅛" wide and then apply silicone around it to hide their mistake. It looks awful.

The secret here is to determine, and start from, the lowest point. (this is usually at the side of the drain.) That way, you will have a level, clean, even cut at the bottom of the first row of installed tiles.

Tiling around a tub.

So, measure the hight of the tile from the lowest point of the tub—that is your level point. Place your level across that point, mark it, and install the ledger boards, only if you decide to use them.

If you are installing small tiles, like 4" by 4", 6" by 6", or glass tile, it is a good idea to use OmniGrip Maximum Strength Tile Adhesive because it doesn't slip. This is best used with a $\frac{1}{16}$" or ⅛" trowel, depending on how level the walls are. But if walls need leveling, use mortar or thinset to level them. Let the mortar or thinset dry and then install the adhesive and tile.

I like the adhesive on smaller tiles because the work flows faster. The only downside of using adhesive is that it takes longer to dry or cure fully. It usually takes a couple of days to dry before you can grout. Whenever I'm tiling a full shower with adhesive, I let it dry for 2–3 days before grouting. Again, never use wall adhesive for floor installation.

When tiling around tubs, after the temporary ledger board is leveled and installed, and you have figured out the layout, you may wonder where to start tiling. I usually start at the back-end wall and finish that first, then move on to the side walls. This just works best for me. But at this stage, you can start with any wall.

Finished tiling around tub.

SHOWER FLOOR INSTALLATION

When installing shower floor tiles, use the same process: Find the CL. If the tiles are set individually, make sure the pitch of the floor is toward the drain. If the floor is not pitched, you can add mortar at the edges to achieve the desirable pitch. Use fast-setting mortar—it dries in under 15 minutes. Let it dry, then apply waterproof and begin installing. Most professionals usually install the shower floor after they are done with all of the walls, but this isn't strictly necessary. I used to do the floor first, but now I do the floor after the walls are complete because the grout looks much more even. Do not install tiles bigger than 6" by 6" on shower floors. I have replaced floors that had 12" by 12" tiles that broke, and it is hard to achieve the right pitch with them.

You can use 2" by 2" on a net, or 4" by 4" individual pieces, or 6" by 6" tiles, but never 12" by 12" pieces. If you do, you will certainly have problems later on.

When tiles on a mesh are being installed, this can be a little tricky. I measure the floor and then lay down the tile outside the floor and take the measurement, making sure to deduct the thickness of the spacers, and cut them. Then number the tiles

Measuring, numbering and cutting the tiles before installing.

with a marker or tape in the order they were cut and to follow the order they will be installed, just to make installation perfectly. Note, here you do not need to find the CL, just cut one side.

Before setting the tiles, check if they are cut perfectly by laying them in the shower floor.

Now take them out and lay them outside the shower floor. If they are good to go, you can install thinset and the tiles one by one, in the order they were measured and numbered. It will save you more time than if you were to cut them as you set them. Usually, when I install precut tiles, I spread thinset on the whole floor and then install all of the tiles. The result is a perfect, smooth layout.

The average shower floor is 4 ft. by 4 ft., or 16 ft.[2].

BACKSPLASH TILE INSTALLATION

As I explained in the previous chapter, when installing backsplash tiles, you don't need a level board. The countertop should be perfectly level, so start with a full tile and work your way up. Work your CL for symmetrical cuts. If there is a corner wall, I usually start with a full tile on the edges and leave the cuts on the corners. Visualize it in advance.

Install bullnose tile or a metal square/round edge tile edging trim, at open ends of the backsplash and at the top, if there are no upper cabinets for the tiles to butt against. Draw a leveled line at all open ends for a perfect plumb finish. Install a temporary ledger board as a bridge, connecting both ends of counter top, behind the stove to support tiles and to follow a straight line.

When there is an existing backsplash, I cut and change the drywall as well. It is easier and ultimately faster than removing tile by tile and repairing the drywall after. I cut the drywall with a variable-speed oscillating multi-tool on the edges. Carefully cutting both grout and drywall on the edges of the cabinets and countertop, remove it and install new drywall. This works well for me. This is a personal choice, though, so you can use whichever method you feel more comfortable with.

If there is not an existing backsplash, you can tile directly onto the drywall. You do not need to do a thing to the drywall, but just start tiling. Many people install Durock on top of the existing drywall, but you don't need to do this because the tiles don't get exposed to running water or humidity. In fact, if you put Durock on top, it will stick out and give you a hard time on the edges when the tiles are installed. Tiling on the drywall backsplash is okay.

Leveled countertop—work your way up, starting with a full tile.

Metal square edge trim.

Finished backsplash.

6
GROUTING

Grouting is the most exciting step of tiling—this means that the actual tiling process is complete and you are ready for the icing on the cake!

Things you will need for grouting:

- Grouting trowel
- Two - 2-gallon bucket (1 for water) and (1 to mix grout)
- Grout Sponge
- Grout (sanded or non-sanded)
- Grout mix

There are two types of grout: sanded and non-sanded. Which one should you use? If the grout gaps are ⅛" or wider, then use sanded grout. It will fill in better, it will look better, and it will be easier to work with. This includes glass tiles because the sanded grout will not scratch the surface of the tile. Many tile retailers will tell you to use non-sanded grout, which means that the grout does not have sand in it, but I recommend using the non-sanded grout only when the grout gap is $1/_{16}$" or smaller.

Not only can you get grout in sanded and non-sanded forms, but you can also choose either regular grout or premixed grout. With premixed grout, you do not have to seal it. Never use premixed grout on shower floors! I have done many repairs where homeowners or contractors have used this kind of grout, and, because of moisture on the floor, the grout becomes mushy and starts to wash out.

When you read the label on premixed grout, it clearly says not to use it underwater. Although the shower is not technically underwater, there is still enough water to ruin the premixed grout. Instead, you should use grout mix to seal the grout yourself.

So, what is grout mix? Well, as I tell my clients, prior to seven years ago—when we needed to seal the grout by applying sealer to it after it cured (which would take 24–48 hours)—the problem was that the sealer would only last for about 6–12 months. Therefore, the process would have to be repeated periodically. In some instances, people never did seal this grout again; they thought one time was enough. But then wear and tear would occur, and the sealer would wear out, especially when cleaning or scrubbing the tile and grout.

Grout mix is great because if you simply add it to the grout, it will seal the grout for you, avoiding the need to reseal the grout every 6–12 months. When you add grout mix, the grout lasts longer because the seal is within the grout, not just on its surface.

Some grout mix is applied with water; with other grout mixes, you use the grout mix without (or instead of) water. Either type works well. Once you have decided what sort of grout you would like to use—whether sanded or non-sanded, regular or premixed—you are ready to begin grouting.

To start grouting, begin removing all of the spacers. Do not leave or dig in the spacers on the grout lines. (if needed, use a pair of pliers to remove them)

To avoid grout distraction, the grout lines need to be thoroughly clean. Take a utility knife and start carefully removing excess thinset around the edges of the tile. Dig out any filled thinset to make room for the grout. This cleaning process needs to be done the day after tiling. If you wait longer, the thinset will be dry and hard and will become much more difficult to remove.

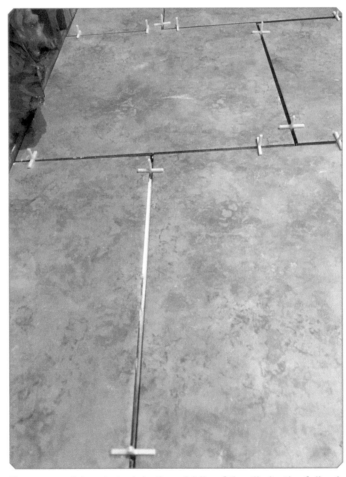

Clean the excess thinset stuck in the middle of the tile by the following day.

Right after removing the extra thinset, get a bucket of water and a grout sponge and start cleaning the edges and the excess thinset left on the tile for a smooth grout layout. If this step is not done prior to grouting, you will have a hard time removing it while the grout is being polished. The excess thinset will show, and it will throw off your grout—your grout work will certainly look bad with thinset on it.

APPLYING SANDED GROUT

Mix the grout in a clean (preferably 2-gallon) bucket. Mix it in a way that is neither too wet nor too dry. Mix it to the consistency of sour cream, remembering to add the grout mix.

Begin applying the grout, making sure all of the grout lines are filled evenly. Try not to leave excess grout on the tiles. The less grout you leave on the surface of tile while grouting, the better. Do this section by section—for floors, you can grout an area of 8 ft. by 8 ft., or up to 10 ft. by 10 ft., at a time.

Grouting by sections.

Fill a 2-gallon bucket with clean water and get a grout sponge. Begin by cleaning the excess grout with the grout sponge in circular motions. This evens out the grout and cleans away the excess. Clean the tiles 3 ft.² at a time. Afterward, rinse the sponge in the bucket, twisting it hard to make sure no water is dripping or left in the sponge. Then clean the same spot you just cleaned, wiping from left to right or right to left. Pass the sponge evenly across the tiles and grout once. Then flip the sponge, pass it across once again, and rinse the sponge again. Do this repeatedly, but do not pass the sponge twice without rinsing it. If you do, any residue from the sponge will then stick back to the grout and tile.

Again, make sure the sponge is not dripping water when you clean the grout. Continue to clean the grout off and change the water as needed. Never dump the grout water in sinks or toilets because it could clog or damage piping. Instead, go outside and dump it somewhere in the back of the house. Then use clean water to gently clean the grout lines again, polishing and removing extra grout that may have been left from the first cleaning. (I call it "polishing" when you clean grout the second time). As you remove any excess grout left on the grout lines, make sure the grout lines appear even and smooth.

After you are done cleaning it the second time, view it at a distance. If you notice that the floor looks a little dusty, get clean water and a clean sponge and clean it once more.

Again, begin with 3-ft.^{2} sections. Begin cleaning from left to right or right to left. Pass the sponge once, flip it, pass again, and then rinse the sponge. Do this until you finish cleaning the whole area and the floor looks dust-free. Then let it sit. Don't walk on it until it dries. It normally cures in 12–24 hours. After it is dry, dust it off—and you are done!

APPLYING NON-SANDED GROUT

Never grout and then leave the grout unclean for too long. Know that non-sanded grout dries faster than sanded grout, so do one wall at a time because non-sanded grout dries faster. Do not leave grout unclean for more than 10 minutes. Once it hardens, excess grout will be difficult to remove.

One of my dearest friends called me one morning and asked about the grouting process because he was removing and replacing his un-sanded wall grout. I told him how to do it, and he said; "That's simple! I got it."

Then I added, "Remember to clean it right away—don't let it sit for more than 10 minutes after it's applied. I can give you a hand if you want."

He said, "No, I got it!"

The following day he called me up and asked, "Rob, how do I clean the grout, and how can I clean it off the walls after it's dry?"

"What happened?" I asked.

He replied, "I did what you told me, but when I was cleaning the grout, it was coming out, so I decided to leave it on longer. I left it on overnight, and now I can't take it out! What do I do now?"

I responded, "There isn't much you can do!" He and his son spent the whole day scraping and sanding it out, but they couldn't get it out completely.

Eventually, one year later, they had to remodel the old tiles anyway. But don't let grout harden, because as it hardens, it becomes harder to remove and may not come out at all.

CAULKING

When you caulk areas where two surfaces join, many people use latex caulk that's matched in color to the grout. To get a good bead, don't open the tube hole too much and be sure to work the caulk into the join carefully and firmly.

Here is a good chance to use the premix grout instead of same-color grout caulk or ceramic tile caulk. I like premix grout better than the same-color caulk on wall corners. Pre-mix grout lasts longer—but not on shower floors.

I do not recommend installing matching latex caulk in the shower corners or on the shower floor because it gets moldy quickly due to the humidity.

APPLYING SILICONE

On tubs, I like to use silicone caulking. Silicone is stronger and will last longer than the same-color grout caulk. The only downside of silicone is that it only comes in three colors: white, bone, and clear. However, I prefer silicone around tubs because there is relatively more movement but silicone is flexible and mold resistant.

When applying either type of caulk, open a small hole in the tube, which will result in a fine line. If you open the caulk hole too wide, the line will come out too thick. I usually cut it ⅛" in diameter; if you need it wider, just recut accordingly.

Also, when applying it, don't press your finger too hard on the silicone. If you do, the silicone will spread too wide. One key to using silicone is, when you lay it down, just polish it with your finger once or twice. It cannot be cleaned with a rag like painter's caulk.

When applying silicone, the trickiest thing is working the corners. First, I apply it on the corners and leave a little tail of about an inch off the corner. Then I connect both corners. This way, when I do the middle between the corners, I don't touch the corners.

I continue applying silicone from the tail I left on the first corner all the way to the other corner. If I apply the silicone at the corners first in this manner, the corners will not be messed up when I apply it to the rest of the lines.

Installing silicone—start at the corners and continue along the lines.

MY EXPERIENCE WITH GROUTING

Since 2000, I had been working for my own company in all phases of home remodeling: kitchens, bathrooms, finished basements, stucco, siding, and roofing. We did it all.

Then I got burned out and wanted a change. I was living in Long Island, NY, at the time, but for a few years, my wife and I had planned to move out of NY. I decided that when we moved, I did not want to continue doing the same kinds of heavy construction. I prayed and asked the Lord to lead me and to give me something else to do.

About two weeks later, as I was coming to one of tile retailers I used to do installations for, I saw someone doing a quick floor demonstration for the store manager on a way to recolor and stain existing grout. After the demonstration, this person—the inventor of the product—asked the store manager, "So, how do you like it?"

The manager replied, "It's definitely a good product, but I'm not interested. Thank you—I wish you good luck." And he walked away.

The store manager wasn't interested because his business was new tile construction, not repairs. But in my mind, I was saying, I think this is what I'm looking for.

As the inventor left the store, I followed. I told him, "That was an awesome demonstration, and it's an awesome product." Though he didn't look too happy after being rejected by the store manager, I got his card.

One year later, in 2007, we were three months from moving when that experience came to mind. I looked for that inventor's card but couldn't find it. So I did some research and found the product already on the market. I ordered a few colors and started to do samples. That was when my new business was born: Grout Solutions

MY COMPANY

After we left Long Island and moved to Georgia, we began Grout Solutions (www.groutsolutions.net).

Before grout coloring came along, when people saw their bathroom floors and showers had cracked or missing grout, their first thought was to remodel and change the tiles. The other option, if they did not have the money to remodel, was to change the grout, either to the original color or to a different color of grout. The only problem was that the process was too dusty because the grout needed to be ground out. It was quite a lengthy, expensive process because you had to be extremely careful not to damage the tile. For this reason, many contractors did not bother with re-grouting.

Removed old grout.

Tile and grout restoration services were not available 10 years ago. Only Grout Solutions and one other company were in business offering that kind of service in 2007.

Grout restored and renewed.

This is what we do: In most cases, the grout is just dirty, worn-out, and stained. When the grout is dirty, discolored, or even damaged, we come in, deep-clean the tile, and replace broken or otherwise damaged grout. After this is deeply cleaned, we apply an epoxy colorant/seal. This colorant comes in a variety of colors, allowing you to match the original color or add a different color depending on your preference.

The result is like a new tiling job! The floor or shower wall tiles look new, refreshed, and clean.

All of the silicone comes out and we install new silicone, making the bathroom look brand-new again without much expense. A lot of people go this route until is time to remodel.

Unfortunately, in some showers where the wrong material was used originally, the only thing to do is a quick repair—or else to remodel the project from scratch.

At least people have a choice now: to invest in a new bathroom or to restore their existing one. At groutsolutions.net, we offer both, restored or new, remodeled bathrooms.

Discolored and damaged grout.

Restored, sealed and stained grout.

45

—— 7 ——
DOS AND DON'TS OF TILING

To conclude this handbook, here is a summary of key dos and don'ts that will help you on your next tile job. Whether you are a homeowner, do-it-yourselfer, novice tile-setter, or tile pro, here are some suggestions based on what has worked for me—and what hasn't:

Don'ts

- Do not install green board on shower walls.
- Do not install drywall screws on Durock.
- Do not install tile adhesive on floors.
- Do not let grout dry before you clean it.
- Do not let un-sanded grout dry for over 10 minutes during installation.
- Do not use tiles bigger than 6" on shower floor.
- Do not leave spacers under grout.
- Do not use Pre-Mix grout on Shower floors
- Do not install durock on shower floor

Dos

- Use Durock on shower walls.
- Fasten underlayment plywood with deck screws.
- Tape shower wall, floor corners, curbs and soap niche
- Waterproof shower walls and shower floor
- Glue Durock against plywood with liquid nails.
- Use proper thinset (rigid).
- Seal grout yourself with grout mix.

AFTERWORD

MY SECRET

Why have I told you my tiling secrets? Because I don't want to keep them to myself. If I can make a job easier for someone else, I will.

Every time I've brought on a new employee, I've taught him all I know. My goal was, and still is, to train others to be better than I am. I always aim to duplicate myself, even if I'm not rewarded financially later on.

As the saying goes, if I offer a man a fish, he'll only be fed for a moment, but if I teach him how to fish, he can feed himself forever. And so it is with tiling. I will be satisfied, and my commission fulfilled, if someone who learned from me says, "Thanks to Rob, I have this skill—I know how to do this now."

Thank you for reading—and happy tiling!

For questions and concerns feel free to contact me at, www.groutsolutions.net
Keep posted for how to Videos coming soon.

Printed in the United States
By Bookmasters